21st Century
Basic Skills
Library

KITS GROW UP TO BE RABBITS

by Cecilia Minden, PhD

Cherry Lake Publishing • Ann Arbor, Michigan

1

Published in the United States of America
by Cherry Lake Publishing
Ann Arbor, Michigan
www.cherrylakepublishing.com

Photo Credits: Cover and page 1, ©Vera Kailova/Shutterstock, Inc.; page 4,
©Arco Images GmbH/Alamy; page 6, ©iStockphoto.com/michicaust;
page 8, ©blickwinkel/Alamy; page 10, ©jokerpro/Shutterstock, Inc.; page 12,
©Megov/Shutterstock, Inc.; page 14, ©Mrmacca/Dreamstime; page 16,
©iStockphoto.com/gallofoto; page 18, ©iStockphoto.com/inhauscreative;
page 20, ©Smit/Shutterstock, Inc.

Library of Congress Cataloging-in-Publication Data
Minden, Cecilia.
    Kits grow up to be rabbits/by Cecilia Minden.
        p. cm.—(21st century basic skills library. Level 1)
    Includes bibliographical references and index.
    ISBN-13: 978-1-60279-854-0 (lib. bdg.)
    ISBN-10: 1-60279-854-0 (lib. bdg.)
    1. Rabbits—Infancy—Juvenile literature. I. Title. II. Series.
    QL737.L32M56 2010
    599.32'139—dc22   2009048571

Cherry Lake Publishing would like to acknowledge
the work of The Partnership for 21st Century Skills.
Please visit www.21stcenturyskills.org for more information.

Printed in the United States of America
Corporate Graphics Inc.
July 2010
CLFA07

TABLE OF CONTENTS

Kits

Kits are baby rabbits.

Kits are born in **litters**.

A litter may have 12 kits.

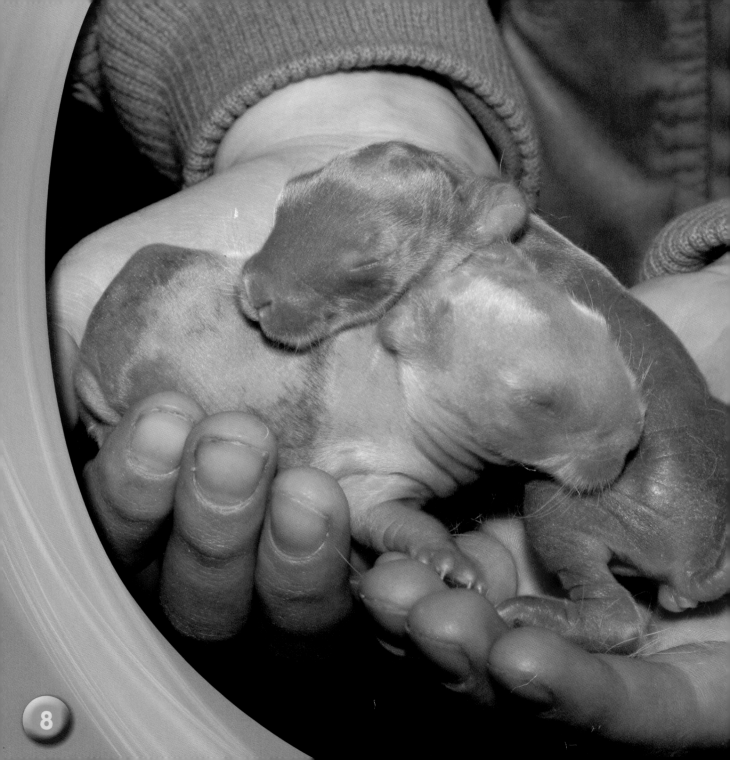

Kits do not have fur.

They cannot see.

Kits like to **burrow**.

This keeps them safe and warm.

Now the kits can see.

Some kits have pink eyes.

Growing Up

Kits get soft fur when they are bigger.

They get out of their nest.

Kits are **fragile**.

Pet them with a soft touch.

Kits like to **nibble** on green plants.

They like to hop and play.

Rabbits

Now the kits are 4 months old.

They are grown-up rabbits!

Find Out More

BOOK

Walker, Kathryn. *See How Rabbits Grow*. New York: PowerKids Press, 2009.

WEB SITE

House Rabbit Society—For Kids
www.rabbit.org/kids/
Find links to rabbit information, videos, and pictures at this site.

Glossary

burrow (BUR-oh) to dig or live in a hole

fragile (FRAJ-il) easily hurt

litters (LIT-urz) groups of babies born to the same mother at the same time

nibble (NIB-uhl) to take small bites of something

Home and School Connection

Use this list of words from the book to help your child become a better reader. Word games and writing activities can help beginning readers reinforce literacy skills.

a	green	nibble	soft
and	growing	not	some
are	grown-up	now	the
baby	have	of	their
bigger	hop	old	them
born	in	on	they
burrow	keeps	out	this
can	kits	pet	touch
cannot	like	pink	to
do	litter	plants	up
eyes	litters	play	warm
fragile	may	rabbits	when
fur	months	safe	with
get	nest	see	

Index

About the Author

Cecilia Minden is the former Director of the Language and Literacy Program at the Harvard Graduate School of Education. She currently works as a literacy consultant for school and library publishers and is the author of more than 100 books for children.